GW00658874

A Tollymore Year
David Kirk

Published by Cottage,
an imprint of Laurel Cottage Ltd.
Donaghadee, N. Ireland 2010.
Copyrights Reserved.
© Text and photographs David Kirk 2010.
All rights reserved.
No part of this book may be reproduced
or stored on any media without the express
written permission of the publishers.
Design & origination in Northern Ireland.
Printed & bound in China.

ISBN 978 1 900935 90 6

Contents

It is not so much for its beauty that the forest makes a claim upon men's hearts, as for that subtle something, that quality of air, that emanation from old trees, that so wonderfully changes and renews a weary spirit

Robert Louis Stevenson

For (in order of appearance!) Ellie, Tom and Alex, Daisy, Poppy and Ruby Rose

Foreword

In 1955 Tollymore became the first Forest Park in Northern Ireland. It was the first time that the gates were opened to encourage the general public to come in and visit the forest environment and enjoy its natural beauty. Tollymore certainly does offer so much in the way of natural beauty, with the backdrop of the Mourne Mountains behind the tree-clad hills of the Drinns and the sound of the Shimna River flowing over the granite boulders scattered along its valley.

Through the year, the variety of colours, shapes and sizes of trees can be seen but spring shows off the variety of flora in Tollymore from the colour contrasts down the Azalea Walk in bloom to the wild bluebell carpets under the newly leafed beech woods.

This flora lays testimony to the long history of Tollymore. Its first written record was in 1611 when King James I of England gave the land to the Magennis family. It was the following century when the First Earl of Clanbrassil, who had married into the Magennis family, started the larger scale planting in Tollymore. In 1930 and 1941 a subsequent heir, the 8th Earl of Roden, sold the Tollymore demesne to what is now the Forest Service.

The multi-purpose forest as it exists today bears testament to Forest Service's commitment to sustainable forest management. Indeed, all Forest Service woodlands, including Tollymore, have been certified under the Forest Stewardship Council Scheme since May 2000, which demonstrates that they are well-managed in accordance with strict environmental, social and economic criteria.

This balanced approach to forest management has delivered the beauty that is Tollymore Forest Park, so wonderfully presented by David through the photographs in this book.

David Small,
Chief Executive Forest Service Northern Ireland

When you enter a grove peopled with ancient trees, higher than the ordinary, and shutting out the sky with their thickly inter-twined branches, do not the stately shadows of the wood, the stillness of the place, and the awful gloom of this domed cavern then strike you with the presence of a deity?

Seneca

Introduction

Like a patchwork blanket, patterned with colours that change with the seasons and the light, stitched with the silver threads of its rivers, Tollymore Forest Park lies draped across the ice-shaped northern foothills of the Mountains of Mourne, a gem of the Irish landscape, rich in secret places and hidden treasures of rock and water and life – and for the young at heart, a magic adventure playground.

Seeking and sharing the company of its trees, to be cheered by the chatter of its dancing waters, or just picnicking in its gardens, taking in the views of spreading forest and curving mountain slopes and thinking 'Wow', more than 200,000 people visit Tollymore every year. Its designation in 1955 as the first forest park in Northern Ireland was an enlightened act – and well-deserved. It is a special place.

And although it is by far the most popular of Northern Ireland's forest parks, with more than 20 miles of gravelled roads winding through its 1,200 acres, and a web of lesser trails and tracks – old paths of deer and badger and fox (and new ones of the trail biker and pony-trekker) – for those wanting to refresh a weary soul, to walk with the spirits of the natural world, finding solitude is never a problem.

Those who know it well would say that Tollymore reveals its best secrets to the walker who leaves the road, plunges in among the trees and explores its quiet places.

But as well as drawing you to its inner secrets, a patch of floral artistry or a bright moss-mantled glade in a dark Tolkien-like cathedral of living columns of Sitka spruce or Douglas fir, Tollymore also draws your eyes outwards and upwards, making you aware of the landscapes around it, pastureland and mountain and distant seas – landscapes that span earth's long history, where rocks that are among Ireland's oldest and those that are its youngest come together and, later shaped by ice and water, create the park's sublime setting.

Exploring the forest you may be lucky enough to see a startled deer and its foal melting away or come across a stag staking its territorial claim in the autumn, or catch a red squirrel or even a pine martin scampering along a branch, but generally the 20 or so species of animals that live their lives in Tollymore get wind of you and slip away long before you get a glimpse of them. But the woodland undergrowth and riverbanks are teeming with life even if many of the creatures are too small to see. Over the years more than 70 species of birds have been recorded in the park.

The hunter-gatherers, from their camps on the nearby Murlough sand dunes, created the first tracks along the Shimna River. When the Neolithic settlers, and their successors using bronze and iron, had cleared the land of the pine, birch and oak that had covered the Mourne foothills and valleys in the warmth following the retreat of the ice, walls were built in its valley to protect them, their animals and their crops. Now slumbering under their mossy blankets, they can still be traced among the trees of Tollymore.

The Park today, with its myriad of habitats, is a creation of man – men and women with the dreams, and the means, to create elegant and gracious surroundings to reflect their social status and exploit the potential of the land, and the generations of those with skill in stone and wood and earth, whose names, never written down, are long lost in the past, but whose hands created landscapes.

The commercial imperatives that prevailed at the time the demesne was acquired for state forestry have not been kind to much of the built heritage of Tollymore but in creating a new landscape and opening up its diversity of habitats it has created a new heritage, as a people's park, offering nature, adventure, excitement and fun to be passed down the generations. Those who enjoyed it as children when the park opened now watch their children's children doing the same, playing among the trees, climbing and exploring, bouldering its rocky rivers – or just jumping into the Shimna's deep cold pools. The magic of Tollymore is strongest when experienced through the imagination of the adventurous.

Schools and youth leaders rightly use it to show children the enchantment of the woods, to teach them outdoor skills – and to appreciate and protect this, their heritage.

This landscape has shown many faces during its long evolution since the great ice sheets melted away, from frozen tundra to primordial woodland, to rough mountain pasture, then farmland, grazing for the deer-herds beside the 'big house' with its manicured pleasure gardens and exotic trees to the commercial cultivation, over more than two centuries, of millions of trees renowned for the quality of their timber – spruce for city houses, larch for the boats that sailed and harvested the seas, oak for the grand staterooms of the Titanic.

Commitment to landscape enhancement and heritage and conservation principles and the improvement of recreation facilities is now written into the management strategy of the Forest Service and is shaping the present and future of Tollymore, but it is still managed primarily as a commercial forest, a role which exemplifies in fact the endlessly repeating cycles of life. A feeling of sadness is unavoidable when the time comes for tall trees felled as they reach maturity leaving acres of what seems like desolation, but the bright green new seedlings that are planted in their place will someday be a new forest of giants for generations not yet born to explore and enjoy.

A Tollymore Year is not a guidebook to the park, or a detailed natural history – it is a ramble through it, and the changing of its seasons, in images and words which hopefully might inspire and create an appreciation of its often unseen charms – charms that are there to be discovered by those who seek them. Hopefully it will also encourage an appreciation of all such amenities and the importance of cherishing and protecting them.

Hi there – welcome to Tollymore!

It is not so much for its beauty that the forest makes a claim upon men's hearts, as for that subtle something, that quality of air, that emanation from old trees, that so wonderfully changes and renews a weary spirit

Robert Louis Stevenson

The Pleasure Garden lawns framed by the multi-coloured trees of the arboretum

Gardens that remain a pleasure

The pleasure gardens that once created a stylish setting for the 'big house' at Tollymore and on which much loving care was lavished by successive owners continue to be enjoyed today as the lawns and collection of exotic trees surrounding the main car park, where the house stood. It was demolished in the early 1950s. The seven-acre arboretum that forms the background to the 'formal' recreational areas of the Park is the oldest such collection of exotic trees and shrubs in Ireland, the first having been planted in 1752. Age and strong winds have reduced the number of its trees – at one time it contained 65 deciduous and more than 110 conifers – but there are still many impressive, even majestic, specimens. (Considerable extra interest would be added if the practice of labelling the trees was revived!).

West of the present gardens area lies a chequerboard of quarter-acre squares of ground separated with walkways laid out in the 1960s. These were 'trial plots', a research and demonstration project involving some 90 species of trees to assess their potential for commercial forestry or amenity planting. Today, especially in the spring and autumn, they provide a varied patchwork of form and colour to wander among, ranging from multi-patterned eucalyptus to silver birch and giant redwoods.

The stately Cedar of Lebanon which stands proudly at the corner of the car park like a doorkeeper to Tollymore

The Heart of the Tree

What does he plant who plants a tree?
He plants the friend of sun and sky,
He plants the flag of breezes free,
The shaft of beauty, towering high,
He plants a home to heaven ahigh
For song and mother-croon of bird
In hushed and happy twilight heard-
The treble of heaven's harmony
These things he plants who plants a tree.

Henry Cuyler Bunner

You have to book early to get a pitch during the summer in Tollymore's beautifully situated camping and caravan site

A Red Admiral – one of a wide range of butterflies to be spotted among the wild flowers

I saw autumn in the misty morn stand shadowless in silence, listening to silence.

Thomas Hood

Probably the most iconic and cherished feature of Tollymore's built heritage, Foley's Bridge was built in 1787 by James Hamilton, the Second Earl of Clanbrassil who, over 40 years of creative energy, built the foundations of the present park. A light-hearted whimsy with a decidedly Alpine look, the bridge, named after a niece of his wife, is one of five the Earl built as he developed the estate into one of the finest demesnes in Ireland – as well as a successful commercial enterprise

This ghostly ruin, of which only the entrance arch remains standing among the trees about 750 metres west of the car park, was of the same era as Foley's Bridge – built on what at the time was open land for a purpose that is a tantalising mystery (possibly a shelter for deer-hunters, or a stable). The stones of the other three walls of the 30 by 15 ft building lie scattered in mossy tumbles and shrouded in vegetation

I am the heat of your hearth,
The shade screening you from the sun;
I am the beam that holds your house,
The board of your table;
I am the handle of your hoe,
The door of your homestead;
The wood of your cradle,
And the shell of your coffin.
I am the gift of God
And the friend of man.

Anonymous

Each autumn spreads a new carpet of
golden leaves through the woodland

Three sets of strategically placed stepping stones offer dry and convenient ways to cross the Shimna – when storm waters streaming off the mountains do not submerse them too!

Tollymore's 20 miles of gravelled tracks – and many lesser winding ways – lure the walker to explore the ever-changing woodland

The woods are lovely, dark and deep

Robert Frost

Then long-awaited and lovely Spring throws open the doors for another annual performance of life and colour

Rhododendrons scatter their blooms to spread the red carpet for visitors to Tollymore.

The waters, and at times the ice, streaming down from the Mourne Mountains, have spent millions of years sculpting the landscape of Tollymore

The forested slopes of Tollymore lie tucked in below the high slopes of the northern Mourne Mountains.

The Setting
A landscape sculpted by time

Driving southwards, with the high Mountains of Mourne looming larger and larger, the twin summits of The Drinns, the saddle-shaped ridge which defines the shape of Tollymore Forest Park, remain coyly hidden among the folds of the County Down countryside.

Rising steeply from the banks of the Shimna River, The Drinns – the word means 'divided ridge' – nestles at the feet of its big brethren as if for protection, and in a way Tollymore gets it, as the high mountains capture the waters of the wet south-westerly winds that blow most of the time, giving the land in their lea a lower than average rainfall. The downside however is that the clouds created by the air rising over the mountains deprive the park of a lot of sunshine, but it doesn't seem to mind.

It is ironic however that Northern Ireland's heaviest ever day of rain was recorded in Tollymore on October 31, 1968, when 160 mm fell on the northern foothills of the mountains – the Shimna River that day must have been a torrent to behold!

Tollymore is a tranquil place today – and it is hard to imagine it as a battlefield of the gods. But for tens of millenia it was, as great glaciers flowing from high mountain corries fought for possession of the slopes and valleys with invading ice sheets – at times thicker than the mountains were high – grinding their way first from the north and later from the west. Alternately advancing and retreating their jousting created the beguiling landscape that is the setting for Tollymore.

About 15,000 years ago the glaciers withdrew to their mountain corries and the ice sheets melted away, their rapid departure raising sea levels many metres higher than today. When life returned to the warming land the waves would have been breaking near to Tollymore's eastern boundary but then, relieved of its burden of ice, the land began slowly to rise too from the sea and the waves retreated to the present shoreline.

Melting away the ice left the valleys and plains with a deep mantle of drift, mineral-rich clays and gravels (excellent as it proved for the growing of tall strong trees) through which the Shimna and the other rivers cut their way down through until they reached the solid bedrock again and began sculpting the dramatic gorges and pools and cascades that are such a feature of Tollymore.

The rock foundations of the park's scenery span more than 350 million years of earth history and tell again of mighty forces in action, of continents colliding and continents splitting apart. Deep seabed sands and silts trapped between two continents as they drifted into each other and joined more than 400 million years ago were crushed, hardened and concertinaed into the Silurian slates and shales that underlie most of County Down and from which the valleys and hills are sculpted. Their banded, folded strata can be seen all along the Shimna.

Tollymore's dramatic backdrop had similar dramatic origins, but this time the tectonic forces were tearing the continent apart again. The shining granites from which the Mountains of Mourne are carved rise out of the ancient shales just a few hundred metres from the park's southern boundary wall. Sixty million years ago this granite magma surged up to harden in voids in the ancient rock as the continent was stretched and split, giving birth to the Atlantic Ocean. Many dykes hardened from magma that filled the cracks in the splintering earth's crust are also revealed along the river courses.

Old Scots pine and beech guard Tollymore's southern boundary from where the moorland starts its sweep up to the mountains

Enter these enchanted woods, you who dare

George Meredith

The course of the Shimna River can be traced running down through Tollymore from the top right of this aerial picture. To the south, (on the left) its commercial plantations clothe the steep hill ridge called The Drinns and to the right lie the open parkland, the Pleasure Gardens and the arboretum

Caravans sprinkle the spaces between the sheltering trees

In the world there is nothing
more submissive and weak
than water. Yet for attack-
ing that which is hard and
strong nothing can surpass it.

Lao-Tsu
Chinese philosopher
(6th century BC).

Laid down as beds of mud and silt on an ancient
seafloor, the collision of two continents more than
400 million years ago left them hardened, folded
and contorted. The Silurian shales as they are known
underlie most of County Down and carving its valley
round the flank of the much younger but more resist-
ant granites of the Mourne Mountains the Shimna
River has eroded them away – and continues to deep-
en its channel, revealing, shaping and polishing them

North from Tollymore's heights is a panorama of field and forest and granite hills. In the distance the historic town of Castlewellan is backed by the tree-covered hills of its own Forest Park, and beyond them the serrated skyline of Slieve Croob's ancient granites – close neighbours of the Mournes – but 350 million years older

Visitors to Tollymore enter through the stern Barbican Gate, (Barbican refers to the type of design, an archway between two towers) built around 1780 and inspired, like most of his other structures, by the Second Earl of Clanbrassil's English architectural guru Thomas Wright. The gate opens into the long avenue of majestic Himalayan (or Deodar) Cedars, which were planted about 60 years later

A red valerian splashes colour in one of the trefoil 'windows' in the gate's towers

In contrast to the no-nonsense Barbican, the Bryansford Gate, built as the main entrance to the demesne a few years later but now the point of departure from the Park, is an elegant statement of grandeur, again inspired by Thomas Wright. Unfortunately, driving out of the park you have your back to the scene. Looking south it beautifully frames the promise of what Tollymore offers, as the following picture shows

The view looking south from the Bryansford Gate

It is situated in the midst of the most sublime scenery with the wide expanse of ocean open before it; yet nowhere do the trees grow with greater luxuriance. Through this delicious spot rush the assembled mountain rivulets, creating in their passage, cascades of every variety of force and form. It is scarcely possible to imagine a scene where natural beauties and advantages have been turned to more valuable account by judgment, skill and taste, than this, which lies as the foot of Slieve Donard and almost on the brink of the ocean.

Mr & Mrs Hall, Travelling in Ireland 1840

Climb the tracks winding up the hills known as the Drinns you can look down on the arboretum, with its many shapes of trees and colours changing through the year, with the car park on the right and Bryansford village behind

Tollymore's colourful Azalea Walk leads the eye to the forested slopes of the Drinns and the soaring Mountain slopes behind.

Looking north from the heights of the Drinns

Give me a land of boughs in leaf,
A land of trees that stand;
Where trees are fallen, there is grief;
I love no leafless land.

A.B. Housman

Winter
—the Sleeping

Spring frolics with its flowers and bird-song, summer struts its opulence, autumn amazes with its colourful display but winter, when forest life is largely dormant and the sun barely manages to peep over the mountains, can transform Tollymore's time of quiet contemplation with days of beauty and drama that will sparkle in the memory like no other.

The ultimate winter wonderland experience, when trees and tracks are blanketed in deep soft snow, the only sound the crunch of your footsteps, is rarer now than even a few decades ago; changing climate patterns give us maybe only one or two days in a winter when the forest is transformed, but when it does – be there for the magic of it!

But even clear nights with chilled air flowing down the slopes can transform the forest with frost, framing the river boulders with rims of ice and the leaves of the track-side shrubs and grass hoary white. At other times walking among the tall trees as they sway and thrash in the winter gales coming round the mountains is an experience to remember.

Stripped down to their bare limbs as if for a shower

after their long summer of warm work the great trees create scenes of dramatic grandeur silhouetted against the soft pearly skies that only winter brings, or against a sultry sunset.

Although many of the creatures and most of the plants and trees snuggle down in hibernation to get through cold dark months, the woodland still teems with life, from the millipedes and woodlice that graze the vertical pastures of green algae coating the bark of the bare trees to the foxes, badgers and squirrels that forage for the sparse rations. The dearth of insects, most of which hibernate or spend the winter as pupae hidden under the deep leaf litter of the woodland floor makes winter a famine time for birds, many of which sadly succumb before reaching the Spring.

WINTER TREES

No rustle now
of leaves green
or falling gold.
Summer's sun harvested
the trees strip down
for their winter break;
stem, branch and twig revealed,
fractal sculptures
that sigh, or roar, with the wind,
and filter pastel light.

Beings, proud,
of awesome strength
or fragile grace,
their true beauty bared
in patterns
of incomprehensible
complexity.

Through the short cold days
they wait,
pondering their
long slow lives
and all the life
they draw around them;
wait to sense
the lengthening of the light
and feel again the thrill
of spring's first surging pulse.

David Kirk

I frequently tramped eight or ten miles through the deepest snow to keep an appointment with a beech-tree, or a yellow birch, or an old acquaintance among the pines.

Henry David Thoreau (1817-1862)

The incomprehensible complexity of the pattern of bare tree limbs against the winter sky

The dynamic nature of our landscapes is demonstrated by the way in which in a matter of minutes a river bank and the man-made path along it can be washed away by the river's winter torrent.

A society grows great when old men plant trees whose shade they know they shall never sit in.

Greek Proverb

There is nothing in the world more beautiful than the forest clothed to its very hollows in snow. It is the still ecstasy of nature, where every spray, every blade of grass, every spire of reed, every intricacy of twig, is clad in radiance

William Sharp

Whitebeam berries shine in the winter rain

The trees along Tollymore's mountain boundary strip down to face the winter gales roaring down from the mountains

Winter, a lingering season, is a time to gather golden moments, embark upon a sentimental journey, and enjoy every idle hour.

John Boswell

Trees are the best monuments that a man can erect to his own memory. They
speak his praises without flattery, and they are blessings to children yet unborn.

Lord Orrery, 1749

Winter-clothed mountain slopes seem to call to those walking Tollymore's tracks

I prefer winter and fall, when you feel the bone structure of the landscape – the loneliness of it – the dead feeling of winter. Something waits beneath it; the whole story does not show.

Andrew Wyeth

Tollymore's giant beeches filter the pastel winter light

Between every two pines is a doorway to a new world

John Muir (1838-1914)

A series of violent storms during the 1950s wreaked terrible damage across the forests of northern Britain including those in the north and west of Northern Ireland but Tollymore escaped comparatively lightly, with most of its plantations being only recently planted. It has suffered more from the changing weather patterns of recent years, with winter winds funnelling down the Shimna valley in 2006 and 2007 taking down hundreds of now mature trees and acres of forest subsequently having to be clear-felled before their time. A number of the biggest and oldest of the Park's beech trees have fallen to the winds – fortunately no-one was crossing this bridge in the pleasure gardens at the time!

Violent winds, an increasing occurrence with the pattern of climate change, can take a heavy toll of the plantations – and create problems of tree extraction

Winter is also the time when life is at its lowest ebb and trees are dormant, for forestry operations to reach their peak, the felling of trees whose time has come, and the planting of the next generation. Depending on the species of tree and the quality of growing conditions most commercial plantings follow a 50 to 70 year cycle

Felled trees lie ready for collection by the roadside while already the newly planted saplings wait to burst into growth in the spring – the next generation

**Ghosts of the world-wood: the trees are felled,
Stumps; puny saplings which replace them
will outgrow me and then outlive me.**

Michael Vince, 'The Thicket'

Piled logs await removal to the sawmill

Early snows clothe the ground before the trees
have finished shedding their green leaves

This patch of snowdrops in the arboretum has been spreading and heralding the end of winter in Tollymore for more than 100 years

The flowers of late winter and early spring occupy places in our hearts well out of proportion to their size

Gertrude S Wister

Trees
worth knowing

With its arboretum, its 92 demonstration plots and its patchwork of commercial plantings Tollymore has probably the widest range of tree species of any park in Ireland. With age and storm taking down many of its finest specimens over the years, such as the famous Seven Sisters, a group of giant Silver Firs, it can boast only two record breakers – a *Eucalyptus gigantea* which holds the Irish girth record for its species and a Honda spruce *(Picea jezoensis)* which is Irish champion for both girth and height (both in the arboretum). Biggest arboretum tree is the Giant Redwood (Sequoia) which is pushing 120 feet but in terms of an impressive presence its nearby neighbour, the Monterey pine, is hard to beat. But all through Tollymore, even in the conifer plantations where many long-surviving broadleaved trees have been planted round, there are magnificent trees, tall, old, gnarled and twisted with age, with beards of moss, elegant and airy. Trees worth getting to know.

Oak – the strong one

The stands of great oaks in Tollymore planted in the 18th century, whose timber was chosen for the carvings and the grand staircase of the Titanic and to panel the walls of many stately homes, are no more, but individual specimens, scattered throughout the Park often in the shade of the newer conifer plantations, are now the venerable sages of the woods, their wide-stretching boughs bearded with moss and ferns.

Oaks live longer than any other native tree except the yew, sometimes more than 1,000 years, provide stronger timber, and host a greater richness of wildlife than any other, providing shelter and food for hundreds of organisms from birds and squirrels, insects from beetles to mites and many algae and fungi. And the older they are the greater the diversity.

The old oaks of Tollymore have stood, some with the Shimna waters washing their feet, for more than two centuries, witnessing the cycles of many seasons and many generations of men and of the trees from foreign lands planted that now keep them company.

Then here's to the oak, the brave old oak,
Who stands in his pride alone!
And still flourish he a hale green tree
When a hundred years are gone!

H. F. Chorley. 1831-1872

ODE TO AN OLD DEAD OAK

It must have been a terror wind
that brought you down,
A venerable giant
It must have been a mighty crash.
Was anyone there to hear your fall?

No sap rose that Spring,
No leaves unfurled to seek the sun,
No birds came to nest.

But as the sculptor chisels the outer
layers
to reveal his vision,
Through uncounted years
the lives we call decay worked to bring
your inner strength to light.

Smoothed to their hardened core
your wind-curved branches reach out
as if for a last embrace.

The straight lines of straight new trees
planted around you, now tall,
stand vigil in reverence,
protecting a fallen warrior.
There is beauty in the end-
ing of your days.

David Kirk

Canst thou prophesy, thou little tree,
What the glory of thy boughs shall be?

Lucy Larcom, 1826-1893

Regal beech – Queen of the woods

If the oaks are the patriarchs of the woodland, the beech is the queen – tall, elegant, regal – and often with her young ones around her feet. She brings the freshest green brightness to spring and is the greatest glory of the autumn colour – a colour that lasts all winter as her leaves carpet the ground. Even with their leaves cast off, he bare boughs bring an awesome drama to the pale winter skies

Originally grown mostly closely together in plantation conditions (as new ones still are, covering many acres north of the river), Tollymore's old beeches have grown tall and straight – smooth soaring columns with crowns high above. Because they come into leaf comparatively late the spreading bluebells and other spring plants have time to grow and flower before the summer puts a roof on the living cathedral. Every leaf of a beech tree gets a share of the light but little gets through to the ground below!

Beech does not enjoy the longevity of oak, rarely living more than 150 to 200 years. Being shallow-rooted they are susceptible to drought and in maturity their height and heavy crowns and a tendency for their heart-wood to rot make them easy victims to violent winds. Tollymore has lost some fine specimens in the gales of recent years, but many majestic giants remain, thrusting above their neighbours, impressive sights through all seasons of the year.

Larch
– frolicsome and fresh

Praise be for the lovely larch. The other conifers that mainly clothe the slopes of Tollymore, sulky spruce, the formal firs, take themselves so seriously – it's all business with them.

The larch in contrast seem almost frolicsome, enjoying life and bringing colour and brightness. Breaking ranks with other conifers it is Europe's only native deciduous one, the fresh pale green of its spring branches, with their pink and green flowers, washes across the forest creating a patchwork of contrasting shades, and after blending with its neighbours for the summer the pattern is repeated in autumn, but this time in pale yellow, before fading to the orange-brown of winter's bare stems.

Losing its leaves in winter and, when mature, waving its feathery crown in the wind high on straight bare trunks, it allows light and life onto the ground at its feet which other conifers cannot do.

It's not by chance that so much of Tollymore is given over to larch. It is one of the straightest, strongest and enduring and therefore valuable of softwood timbers, superb for structural works and Tollymore's fine specimens were used widely in the building of craft from fishing boats to frigates. Since it started being planted in the park nearly 300 years ago the gentle damp climate and deep, well-drained glacial soils of the northerly slopes have been producing larch of a quality unmatched anywhere else in the British Isles.

Far from their native Australia and Tasmania stands of Eucalyptus, the most light-hearted of all trees, bring year round brightness to the woods; even in winter their multi-coloured, patterned bark sounds a cheerful note

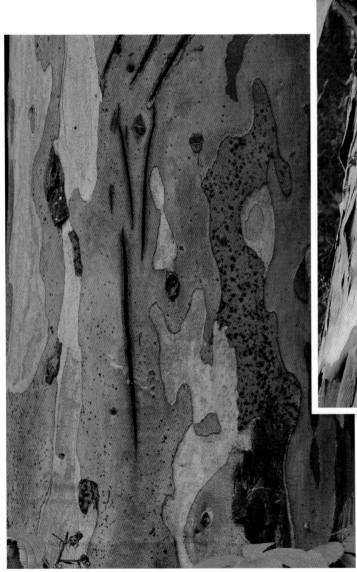

The venerable ones

Venerable old trees, and you encounter many of them as you explore Tollymore's reaches, are habitable universes for a huge abundance of other beings and even invaluable refuges for rare or threatened species – especially fungi, lichens, insects and bats – veritable reservoirs of biodiversity.

The older trees are, the greater the quality and diversity of wildlife they offer refuge to. A fallen log can sustain many life-forms for between five and 20 years before it has been consumed, a living but ageing tree can take a century to slowly die. The dead wood in its centre may be riddled with beetle burrows and as the live outer trunk continues to grow so does the column of dead wood inside. Rugged bark and softened wood also allow other plants, mosses, ferns and even flowering plants, to take hold and flourish high above the ground. The reaching boughs of many of Tollymore's old oaks are veritable jungles of smaller plants.

Old trees frequently have lost branches or other damage which provides access to the hollow interior for flies and wasps and holes for birds and bats to make homes in (some 20 bird species regularly nest in tree hollows). Old and dying trees provide micro-habitats for a breathtaking range of organisms – it is estimated that 40 per cent of woodland wildlife is dependent on them.

A **riverside oak,** one of Tollymore's patriarchs, reaches out with gnarled limbs

Ivy – the eternal opportunist!

Bark – nature's palette of textures

Thick chunky barks, thin smooth barks, twirly barks, multicoloured barks, barks that peel off in strips or plates – every species of tree in Tollymore has a distinctive and recognisable skin.

Ironically the skin we can see and touch – yes, hug it if you want to – is mostly made up of dead stuff – it's a suit of armour to protect the thin layers of living cells behind it where the real business of growing timber goes on, pumping up fluids and nutrients, delivering sugars down to the roots. It's the primary defence against bacteria, fungi, insects, rabbits and grey squirrels, even deer, although when times get tough in winter they'll chew their way through it, possibly killing the tree. Some trees, like the Cork Oak and the Giant Redwood in the arboretum have thick barks designed to enable the tree to survive forest fires.

But apart from offering a valuable tree identification kit and in some cases earning the tree's keep for its own ornamental value, it's interesting stuff and provides a habitat for a myriad of other creatures which hide, sleep, breed, raise families and eat each other in its fissures and crevices.

The main picture (left) shows the wonderful spiralling texture of a Spanish (or Sweet) Chestnut. The montage shows some of the wonderful diversity of tree barks.

As the poet said – Only God can make a tree – probably because it's so hard to figure out how to get the bark on.

Woody Allen

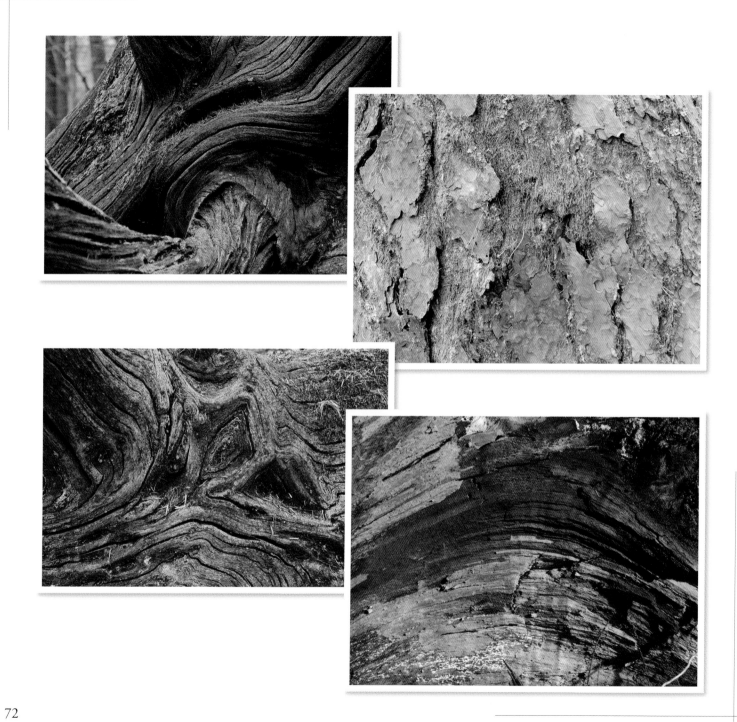

The Yew – dark with inner beauty

Dark shapes by the riverside paths and brooding shadows among the spring and autumn colours of other trees, the Yew, the 'immortal one', is the Darth Vader of the woods.

Moody and enigmatic, the yew is among the longest living of trees and although the oldest of the many in Tollymore are less than three centuries old, specimens in Britain are believed to be as much as 2,000. They are also among the slowest growing of trees – some even stop growing at all for decades before resuming.

The yew has had a spiritual, almost supernatural, reputation since before recorded history. Its nickname as the 'graveyard tree' because of the practice of planting it beside church buildings reflected the pre-Christianity belief that it defended the living and the dead from evil spirits.

But while all parts of the yew are poisonous (except to goats and deer) it is a tree that well deserves a hug. As well as having one of the most variable and adaptable growth modes of

any tree, its black-green foliage is counter-pointed by the multi-coloured fluted sculpting of its trunk and its autumn seed-cases scattered like bright red stars. And its timber is the most beautiful of any native tree, banded in shades from ivory to salmon pink and purple and finishing the smoothest silky sheen – wood-turners in particular will travel a long way to get pieces from a felled tree!

As well as the 'normal' English yew Tollymore has some fine specimens of the multiple-stemmed Irish yew variation – like all their kind descended from a single specimen discovered on Cuilcagh Mountain in Fermanagh in 1770.

Autumn and the red seed casings splash
brightness on the sombre yew

Bowls turned by the author from
colourful Tollymore yew wood

Himalayan (or Deodar) Cedars

The magnificent avenue of Himalayan (or Deodar) Cedars that stand like a guard of honour to welcome visitors to Tollymore stretches for half a kilometre along the driveway from the Barbican Gate. Planted by the Third Earl of Roden in about the 1840s shortly after the trees were first introduced to Britain they then lined the main driveway that ran through open park land with a 26 acre deer park on the south side where the animals could be watched from the big house.

Some of the trees have developed magnificently
outlandish shapes – they seem to cheer you by

Sitka Spruce – a great tree with a bad name

Although it is the tree that gets commercial forests a bad name, covering hillsides with dense blocks of impenetrable darkness, when allowed to mature and given space the Sitka spruce, from Alaska, can be one of the most magnificent of trees.

The biggest of the spruces (and the third tallest of all conifers), it can grow, given a chance, up to 50 metres – and on the low damp riverside ground where it does best Tollymore has produced some fine specimens, huge columns with their distinctive flaking bark and huge root buttresses covered with emerald moss, creating a truly Tolkien atmosphere. Sadly in commercial tree growing size does matter so these giants may not be allowed to survive for long. It would be a heritage asset to the park if a few were left to be admired.

Sitka can be identified by its bark which flakes off in thin discs

A stand of **birch trees** in the demonstration plots turns bright orange in autumn

… trees that are their own sunset

Andrew Young; The Birchwood

Planted close together trees strain upwards to get their share of the precious light, resulting in the development of tall straight trunks with fewer side branches and knots in the timber

An ancient Scots pine reaches for the sky

**I love to lie, when lulling breezes stir
The spiry cones that tremble on the fir**

J Leyden (Noontide)

The **Cork Oak,** from Portugal, one of the best known trees in the arboretum, could be up to 200 years old. With rugged bark of thick cork it is only about 30 feet high but has a spread of almost twice that

The woods decay, the woods decay and fall

Tennyson

A limb, long fallen across the river, has been stripped and polished by the surging waters of the Shimna in spate

A clump of early bluebells herald the bursting of spring colour

Spring
—the Awakening

A long winter sleep over each year's cycle of awakening, feeding and growing begins for the trees and shrubs and flowers and mosses, insects, birds and animals. The majestic beeches and venerable oaks, and the smaller trees, birch, hazel, ash and many more, all jostling for the light, burst into an explosion of bright fresh leaves ready for the serious business of harvesting the summer's sun. The regiments of larch paint wide swathes of cheerful green freshness across the hundred of acres of sombre conifer plantings. Grabbing the light before the leafy canopy closes over the spring flowers, wood anemone, wild garlic, celandine, sorrel, primrose and many others sparkle among the remnants of last autumn's leaf-fall. And for a few short weeks of course the glorious spreading bluebells drift like smoke across the greening earth between the bare tree stems.

Spring life in the woodland is perfectly co-ordinated. The plants time their flowering to take advantage of the frenzy of insect activity on which most of them depend for their pollination. The insects are also the food supply for most birds at the time they need it most.

Above you the woods fill with a cacophony of birdsong as in their thousands, of many species, sometimes almost deafeningly trying to out sing each other, they launch into their rituals of spring, winning mates, building nests and rearing their young, from the ecstatic exuberance of the blackbird to the seductive coo of the pigeon.

The bright sprays of leaves and the flowers of the larch, large red female, tiny male, herald the bursting of spring across Tollymore's plantations

Spring is when life's alive in everything

Christina Rosetti

The first tiny flash of green heralds the coming leaf-burst of spring

Lo! in the middle of the wood
The folded leaf is woo'd from out the bud
With winds upon the branch, and there
Grows green and broad, and takes no care,
Sun-steep'd at noon, and in the yellow moon
Nightly dew-fed; and turning yellow
Falls, and floats adown the air.

Tennyson (The Lotus-Eaters)

Horse chestnut leaves are
among the first to unfurl

A dung beetle goes about its
business of the new year

Keep a green tree in your heart and
perhaps a singing bird will come.

Chinese proverb

Spring is Nature's way of saying 'Let's Party'

Robin Williams

Small is beautiful

The mountains and sky, the bright spring colours, the dark brooding conifer woods, the swirling, dancing waters – the scenery of Tollymore is stunning, but things don't have to be big to be beautiful. Open your eyes to them and the patterns of colour and shape and texture that wood and stone and the colonies of the tiniest living things have as much to offer as the mightiest of nature's displays.

The textures and patterns of tree bark, each one different, 'flowers' of ice crystals on a frozen leaf, islands of multi-textured and multi-coloured lichen on the stones of a wall, and where it is shadier tiny forests of soft emerald moss, late falling leaves scattered on the snow, the river bed's water-sculpted stone, the living rock split by a living tree root, a shaft of sunlight shining through a fresh green leaf, delicate grasses swaying in the breeze, the intricate seed-heads of the dandelion or the willowherb, a dew-spangled spider's web or a water-drop on a bright berry – get down among it and explore the world of the beautifully small …

Spring has returned. The earth is like a child that knows poems.

Rainier Maria Rilke

Ferns – gentle but tough

With their delicate feathery appearance, shepherd's crook growing fronts uncurling in spring and light bright colours early in the year the ferns that brush your legs throughout Tollymore's open woodland seem a delicate member of the plant community – but they're as tough as old boots (unsurprisingly seeing they are descendents of the plants that ruled the planet for millions of years before trees or flowering plants were thought of). It is aggressively invasive given the right soil and the damp shaded conditions it enjoys but fortunately it's an asset to the woodland scene, mixing well with flowering plants and mosses to create some of Tollymore's most delightful scenes.

Ferns die back in winter, snuggling down to survive the cold under their own dead fronds. At their peak in high summer most species do best under woodland canopy and would not survive in the open. And not all ferns are ground-dwellers – look up at some of the venerable old trees by Shimna's banks; their gnarled limbs are veritable hanging-gardens of moss, lichen and ferns growing from the forks and cracks in the bark.

Poor dear silly spring – preparing her annual surprise

Wallace Stevens

Bluebells – spreading joy

Whatever your favourite season of the year might be bluebells drifting like smoke through a dappled wood, as spring begins to turn to summer and before the leafy canopy darkens the ground, must be treasured as one of the most delightful highlights of the Tollymore year.

Bluebells and other flowering plants such as wild garlic, wood anemone and wood sorrel have adapted by being able to blossom in the narrow window between when days warm and lengthen and the leaf canopy above darkens the woodland floor.

Wide swathes of bluebells brighten a spring walk all through the deciduous plantations of Tollymore and the sharp eye will often see white and pinks varieties. While walking through the sea of blue is an enjoyable experience, the flowers suffer from being tramped on – and do not enjoy being picked!

Bluebells propagate by seed and once the flowers have faded they spend the summer building up the strength of the bulbs that will wait out the winter below the soil, protected from frost and trampling feet, ready for the next spring – and another magic display.

Reading about nature is fine, but if a person walks in the woods and listens carefully, he can learn more than what is in books, for they speak with the voice of God

George Washington Carver (1864-1943)

The first of the spring flowers – the wood sorrel

The Sparkling of Flowers

The bluebells do tend to steal the show in late spring but although more scattered between the trees and seldom forming drifts (with the exception of fairly isolated spreads of wild garlic) many other flowering plants rush to grab the light of lengthening days before the awakening trees cut it off again – wood anemone, wood sorrel, primrose, celandine, sparkle among the grasses, mosses and early ferns.

The dainty early spring flowers are mostly white and yellow because the insects they depend on for fertilisation mostly have eyes sensitive to these colours; bees, hover-flies and other summer flyers are more sensitive to blues and reds which are the dominant colours of later flowering plants such as foxglove, willowherb and thistles.

Naturally the areas of semi-open deciduous woodland are the richest treasure-houses of wild flowers in Tollymore but wherever the shading canopy is interrupted, by tracks or by the rivers or where trees have been blown down flowering plants will seize the opportunity for light and life. The most amazing swathes of colour sweep across the ground the summer after forest plots have been felled and foxgloves and willowherb cover acres in glorious purple, a sight that helps make up for the demise of the trees.

Swathes of wild garlic and bluebell clothe the woodland floor

The stitchwort

The gentle primrose

Wood anemone

Daffodils dance around the pleasure gardens

The waters of Tollymore

The Waters
of Tollymore

In the old Irish the river we know as the Shimna was *Abhain na Simhne,* the river of the rushes, which seems an unlikely name of the busy stream that squeezes and dances its way through its rocky confines and boulder beds in Tollymore. And indeed until nearly the middle of the 19th century it was called by the more appropriate if less lyrical name of the Hanalock – *Abhain na lag* – River of rocky slabs. However Shimna may have described accurately the less well drained reaches upriver of the Park and especially below it. However, among the foxgloves and many other plants that burst into life following the clearance in 2007 of a dark plantation of 60 year old Sitka spruce alongside the river in the west of the park were healthy beds of – rushes!

Like many other star performers the Shimna River (*'the most romantic stream that ever burst its way through a channel of rock',* wrote travel writer Charlotte Elizabeth in 1837) has humble beginnings – a bog hole on the sides of the broad basin that drains the peaty slopes of the north-west High Mournes. The highest rainfall of the mountains falls on these slopes and to harvest these waters the Shimna's valley was dammed more than a century ago. But the Fofanny reservoir does not take all and meandering north-eastwards between the fields of its broad valley the Shimna grows again, swelled by other mountain streams.

Most of the water that now flows into Tollymore under its western Boundary Bridge has flowed down the steep slopes of three mountains – Bearnagh, Meelmore and Slievenaglogh, all gathered into the Trassey River (*An Treasaigh* – The fierce one) which joins the Shimna about a mile outside the Park. Just inside the Park

Luke's Stream tumbles down in an elegant waterfall beneath Maria's Bridge on its way to join the rush.

Still broad and bounding from rock to rock on a craggy bed the river passes under Parnell's Bridge, built in 1774, where the first hints appear of the drama to come as the fractured, folded ancient bedrock begins to close in and then for the nearly two miles length of the Park choreographs a dance of water cascading over ledges, surging through narrow gorges and tumbling into deep thoughtful pools where blocks of living rock were once torn out by grinding glacier and washed away by the raging meltwaters. In several places the river's flow has been shaped by man creating crossings where the water glides between stepping stones and plunges down to lower levels.

The Meeting of the Waters, about the centre of the park, is where the Cascade River, tumbling down from the great glacial corrie, the Pot of Legawherry below Slieve Commedagh, adds its waters and its energy to Shimna and they flow on, by the fanciful cliff-face Hermitage, below which, on a rocky shelf by a deep cascade-fed pool, the patient angler sits. A short distance down at the wooden Footstick Bridge, where once the waters were dammed and taken to power a saw-mill, it squeezes through a narrow defile and then on to the Old Bridge below which the adventurous young can jump from high rocks into deep pools.

The Shimna then tumbles and glides through the deepest part of its gorge, where the contorted rock walls and upended slabs tell the tale of ancient continents colliding, to the iconic gem of man's mark on this landscape, the eccentrically beautiful Foley's Bridge.

Below the Bridge the river gradually broadens and shallows again and more gently passes under the last of the crossings, the Ivy Bridge, beyond which it flows eventually to the sea in Newcastle, tamed by man, through the levels of its old flood plain marking a time when it meandered and shaped a land lower than it is today.

Apart from powering a saw-mill built in 1828 in the Park, the Shimna once drove flax and corn mills outside its boundaries, and it was harnessed to drive a turbine to provide electricity for one of the first houses in Ireland to have the new form of energy.

The great charm of the demesne lies in the Shimna River. Here is a deep dark pool, overshadowed by high rocky banks, hung with ferns and hawkweeds. There, a waterfall plunges over a ledge of precipitous rocks. Here the stream meanders among the great boulders fringed and crowned with brilliant moss; there, huge pines and oaks and beeches cast dark shadows on the rippling water. There are picturesque bridges swung across deep chasms and romantic grottoes and everywhere there is a verdure and a wealth of vegetation that is truly delightful.

Robert Lloyd Praeger
Official Guide to Co Down 1900

Huge blocks, hurled, as it would seem, by some gigantic arms, lie in the wildest confusion in the bed of the river; while the fantastic shapes assumed by those which line the banks, the variety of lichens and suckers that spring from every fissure, the darkness of the narrow chasm, enlightened by the foam of those dancing, dashing, whirling waters and the grotesque positions into which the overhanging trees have twisted their trunks, generally mantled in ivy – altogether for such a scene of witchery that I only wonder how I dare dishonour it by any attempt at description.

Charlotte Elizabeth Tonna, Travels in Ireland,1837

**... the most romantic stream that ever
burst its way through a channel of rock.**

Charlotte Elizabeth Tonna

Sometimes a filmy veil, sometimes a thunder-
ing torrent, the Cascade River waterfall has its
own viewing platform. The river bed at the top
of the fall was actually 're-engineered' in the
nineteenth century to enhance its height

The delightful waterfall just above Maria's
Bridge on Luke's Stream which drains
the valley between Luke's Mountain and
Clonachullion Hill at its western edge

Technically just a few yards outside the park's
western boundary these moss-draped falls
are a delightful spot to sit by the Shimna

THE RIVER'S TALE

From glacier-hollowed Legawherry,
From haunting Pollaphuca's granite slabs
where Trassey's torrents rise,
From impounded Fofanny's marshy slopes
and from a million lesser seeps and rivulets
the mountain waters
dash glide trickle,
to join in Shimna's dance.

Stitching with silver
the hem of Mourne's
spreading skirt,
Shimna drains the slopes
that once thick ice,
from north and west,
besieged and shaped.

Her waters,
rippling by stone and root,
or resting in deep dark pools,
or cascading
in exuberant flight,
make music for the forest,
and conversation
for the walker by her banks.

Cutting, grain by grain,
her deep ravines,
she opens windows
on earth's ancient past.
Contorted shales,
the heritage of continents colliding;
where hot magma later rent it
hard dykes
now bend Shimna's course.

A river sparkling in eternal youth,
stone beyond age,
shaping each other.

David Kirk

A river does not just happen; it has a beginning and an end. Its story is written in rich earth, in ice, and in water-carved stone, and its story as the lifeblood of the land is filled with colour, music and thunder.

Andy Russell,
The Life of a River

The riverside walk just below the Footstick Bridge

**The song of the river ends not
at her banks but in the hearts
of those who have loved her.**

Buffalo Joe

A still moment of
reflection – or for reflection

Autumn colours warm the still waters of Tollymore's lake. It is actually an artificial lake constructed in the late nineteenth century by damming the course of a small stream and then digging a channel to take water from the upper reaches of the Cascade River more than a mile away. Its purpose was to guarantee a steady water supply to drive the estate's saw-mill, increasingly busy to meet demand for its high-quality timber. The mill, the foundations of which can still be seen, had been operating since 1828 a few hundred yards further downstream powered by two small mill dams, themselves fed by water taken from sluice gates from the Shimna where the wooden Footstick Bridge now crosses

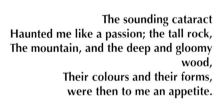

The sounding cataract
Haunted me like a passion; the tall rock,
The mountain, and the deep and gloomy
wood,
Their colours and their forms,
were then to me an appetite.

Wordsworth

The lake provides a sheltered home for a variety
of birds, several species of duck, moor-hen, the
occasional heron and if you're lucky, a kingfisher

109

To those who would listen, the river valley is a magic music box. To those who would observe, the pattern of colour and movement paint a picture that is a masterwork resulting from millions of years of nature's efforts, yet dynamic and ephemeral.

Tom Waters

Another of Tollymore's iconic features – the Meeting of the Waters where the Shimna, flowing round the mountain flanks from the marshy slopes of Fofanny, and already swelled by the waters of the Trassey River tumbling down from Slieve Bearnagh and Meelmore, is joined by the turbulent Cascade, or Spinkwee, River, which drains the great ice-carved bowl of Legawherry

Tollymore's big rivers capture the attention but many small streams splash and chatter their way down to join them along their length

I have never seen a river that I could not love. Moving water … has a fascinating vitality. It has power and grace and associations. It has a thousand colours and a thousand shapes, yet it follows laws so definite that the tiniest streamlet is an exact replica of a great river.

Roderick Haig-Brown

The trees reflected in the river -- they are unconscious
of a spiritual world so near to them. So are we.

Nathaniel Hawthorne

My heart is glad, my heart is high
With sudden ecstasy;
I have given back, before I die,
Some thanks for every lovely tree
That dead men grew for me.

V. H. Friedlaender

Summer
—the Rejoicing

Suddenly it's summer. It often seems a long time coming as life in Tollymore likes to gets the most out of the joys of spring, stretching it out as long as possible!

Then the sun is hot, the skies are blue (well, some of the time) and, the last overwintering bud unfurled, the whole park undergoes an explosion of new greenery that stretches from your feet to the tops of the highest trees. The early spring flowers have faded but the grass verges sparkle with the new ones that like to see the sun on their faces, the daisies, buttercups, speedwells. The shrubbery, rhododendron and fuchsia splash their colour and the warm air carries the scent of the flowers and the breath of the trees.

Overhead, the sprays of leaves turn luminescent as the strong sun shines through and shafts of light shining down through gaps in the canopy create a chequerboard pattern of light and shade on the woodland floor. Small birds flutter through the thickening undergrowth and all around their songs can be heard against the ever-present background of the sound of the river cascading down its rocky bed. In the treetops caterpillars that have been feasting pupate to provide a new food supply for the thousands of birds, both native and foreign visitors.

What were gnarled old trees in their winter bareness suddenly regain their youth and vigour as their leaves burst out to join in summer's opulence. As summer progresses the leaf canopy thickens and the shade deepens but in the open places later flowering plants, foxgloves, willowherbs, thistles and ragworts take to the stage.

Not only nature is in a frenzy of activity at this time – it's high season for all those who enjoy the wide range of recreation activities for which the park is such an unrivalled setting – camping and caravanning, walking, jogging, trail biking and horse riding. The park is also increasingly being appreciated as a superb venue for organised events from vintage car rallies to archery contests.

Spring, being a hard act to follow, God created June

Al Bernstein

Nature doesn't like the desolation that follows the clear-felling of acres of trees any more than we do – and moves quickly to paint it over with colour and new life. Not much grows under the dark canopy but the ground is rich with wind-blown seeds waiting for the chance to burst into life, covering acres with flowers such foxglove, willowherb and ragwort as well as many species of grasses and sedges. The flowers continue to clothe the ground until the new trees grow tall and once again close a shady canopy over them. But they can wait for 60 years until it's their turn again

Trees are poems that earth writes upon the sky,
We fell them down and turn them into paper,
That we may record our emptiness.

Kahlil Gibran

I lean against a birch-tree,
My arms around it twine,
It pulses, and leaps, and quivers,
Like a human heart to mine.

Amy Levy

Rosebay willowherb sprays its late-summer
colour round the edges of the woods

THE DAY THE DRINNS WERE SCALPED

Many a lunch was ate
under the old gnarled
pines and oaks
that crowned the highest
of the ice-smoothed Drinns.
Quare views from there there were,
mountains and sea, forest and farm.

Then from the west, round the mountain flank
a January wind came roaring
and felled the venerable trees,
and many of the younger plantings,
so men came with saws
and scalped The Drinns.

Then they planted new ones,
fir and spruce and larch and pine,
but generations, maybe three or four,
will pass before a lunch will be ate again
under an old gnarled tree on Drinn.

David Kirk

Tollymore's great colour-fest happens in early summer when its collection of rhododendrons down the famous Azalea Walk (now rather a misnomer because all azaleas have been officially reclassified as rhododendrons!). The great froths of exuberant colour put everything else in the shade for a few short weeks

He bestows summer on us and escapes before our realising what we have to thank him for. He doesn't want our thanks.

Robert Frost

Trees

I think that I shall never see
A poem lovely as a tree.
A tree whose hungry mouth is prest
Against the sweet earth's flowing breast;
A tree that looks at God all day,
And lifts her leafy arms to pray;
A tree that may in Summer wear
A nest of robins in her hair;
Upon whose bosom snow has lain;
Who intimately lives with rain.
Poems are made by fools like me,
But only God can make a tree.

Joyce Kilmer

Tollymore is a playground for all ages all year round but naturally all the many activities enjoyed there reach their peak in summer

No traffic hazards here!

Young people set off on an adventure among the trees

God is the experience of looking at a tree and saying 'Ah!'

Joseph Campbell

A peacock butterfly takes a rest

Rhododendron
– a fatal attraction

In 1794 Tollymore was only the second estate in Ireland to be planted with *Rhododendron ponticum,* the newly fashionable shrub of shiny leaves with pretty purple flowers 'imported' into Europe from western Asia and thought to be great for brightening forest tracks and providing shelter for game. It no doubt seemed a good idea at the time. Big mistake. Huge!

As estate owners (or rather their descendents) have since ruefully discovered, *Rhododendron ponticum* is an aggressive alien plague plant – spreading over and through everywhere and smothering any competition, destroying the balance of local plant and wildlife. And with a battery of reproduction and survival techniques it is *very* hard to get rid of. But it has now become more than just a nuisance – it is the main vehicle for the spread of the *Phytopthera ramorum* organism which can kill oak, beech and many other trees and is potentially a bigger threat to our woodlands than the deadly Dutch elm disease.

A programme of ponticum clearance has been under way at Tollymore for the past couple of years, and as a result visitors now have views of the Shimna River's dramatic torrents and pools and water-sculpted rocky course that had in many places been obscured for decades.

It's a pity that it is such a nuisance shrub be-

Rhododendron crowd and colour the Shimna banks

cause in early summer its masses of pale purple flowers are lovely splashes of colour against the dense background of greenery.

Ironically fossil pollen grains have revealed that ponticum was once native to Ireland – 350,000 years ago during a warm period that interrupted the two million year long ice age.

A close relative of *ramorum, Phytopthera lateralis,* is now also causing fatal havoc among Lawson Cypress trees, and the park has lost some of its oldest and biggest in recent years.

This is the forest primeval.
The murmuring pines and the hemlocks,
Bearded with moss, and in garments green,
indistinct in the twilight,
stand like harpers hoar,
with beards that rest on their bosoms.
Loud from its rocky caverns,
the deep-voiced neighbouring ocean speaks,
and in accents disconsolate
answers the wail of the forest.

Longfellow

Among the Trees
of Tollymore

Sunlight brightens the mossy river bank

The mighty buttresses of a mature Sitka spruce offer spreading moss a route up from the forest floor. They have to support a mighty weight with the Sitka reaching maybe 50 metres and having to withstand mighty winds

Mosses – The emerald carpet

Thuidium tamariscinum – now there is a name to conjure with! It's the botanical name for one of the most luxuriant of the many species of mosses flourishing in the damp, semi-shaded conditions that make Tollymore a heaven for these primitive plants. Unfortunately most of them are known only by their Latin names and often telling them apart is a bit of a challenge, but close inspection of their structures will reveal a beauty as fine as any tree.

Spreading like thick soft emerald carpets across the woodland floor, over fallen tree trunks or the scattered rocks of crumbled walls, creating glowing green oases where a dark conifer canopy has a gap, or climbing the lee side of tree trunks, away from the sun and the wind, they are a soothing delight at every turn of a woodland walk.

They don't like hot sun but they do need some light and a lot of moisture. Many grow most actively when it's cool and damp and are at their best in late winter and early spring when they also provide frost protection for flowering plants over-wintering beneath the surface. Related to the very earliest land plants they don't have 'true' leaves, stems or roots and absorb water over their entire surface. The species growing at any location can vary according to differences in the chemistry of the soil and even the water dripping from the trees above.

I have always found thick woods a little intimidating, for they are so secret and enclosed. You may seem alone but you are not, for there are always eyes watching you. All the wildlife of the woods, the insects, birds, and animals, are well aware of your presence no matter how softly you may tread, and they follow your every move although you cannot see them.

Thalassa Cruso

**With gentle hand touch – for
there is spirit in the woods.**

Wordsworth

Why are there trees I never walk under but large and melodious thoughts descend upon me?

Walt Whitman (Song of the Open Road)

A lone fern frond catches a shaft of light breaking through the trees

OF WALLS AND MEN

Walls, their long work long done,
built to tame the hillsides
and feed generations
before history,
lie low, moss- shrouded
between the feet
of Tollymore's tall trees

Walls, of rock hard won,
built with the skill of hands
that did not have the writing
to tell their stories,
are silent witness to lives
long forgotten
as they quietly slumber
and stone by stone
crumble back into the earth.

Walls - step over them
with reverence,
as the spreading forest does,
with thought for those
whose names are lost,
whose heritage they are the bones of.

David Kirk

You will find something more in woods than in books. Trees and stones will teach you that which you can never learn from masters.

St Bernard of Clairvaux

A still pool reflects a patch of sky among the dark conifer woods

An old wooden stairway, an adventure trail and a nature walk for the park's explorers of a century ago that angled up the steep bank from the river to the King's Grave in the west of the park, now sadly abandoned and left to its memories

There's life after death!

Take a wander through the Tollymore woodlands and everywhere you will step over branches and trunks of fallen trees lying on the ground, often moss covered, in various stages of decomposition. Dead wood? Not a bit of it!

Quietly, slowly melting back into the earth from which they grew, these decaying limbs provide habitats for thousand of species of being – fungi, bacteria, lichens, mosses, insects such as beetles and flies, slugs and snails, woodlice and centipedes, which in turn provide sustenance for the small animals and birds that feed on them. The life-cycles of more than 1,700 species of invertebrates depend on decaying wood – in fact there is more life in 'dead' than in living wood!

And of course if it was not for the activities of the insects and fungi, especially the latter, the nutrients locked up in the timber would not be returned to the earth to feed future generations of plants. Even in good conditions of moist shaded ground, it takes up to 20 years for a big log to crumble back into the earth.

Spirit Tree

**In towering splendour once I stood
A regal monarch of the wood,
My branches once reached to the sky
See me now but do not cry.
The Creator's work has yet to cease
I've become a shelter for bird and beast,
And when at last I fall to the Earth
The life I leave will inspire new birth;
A seedling springs forth from the ground
Nature's cycle goes round and round.**

S. Edward Palmer

Life in the treetops

With its mix of broadleaf woodland and dense conifer plantations Tollymore offers the widest possible diversity of habitat for wildlife.

The conifers that cover most of Tollymore's slopes have a reputation as being gloomy, unvarying and inhospitable for wildlife, supporting only a few species compared with the hundreds to be found on an old oak for instance. But this is so wrong. Such forest canopies are now known to be seething with invertebrate life – possibly more than 1,200 individuals or more per square metre – more in fact that will be found on most broadleaved trees such as beech, ash or chestnut. And that of course means they are rich pickings – as well as good shelter and roosting sites – for small birds which, especially during winter, can be seen feeding among them in flocks of many species.

Among the Firs

And what a charm is in the rich hot scent
Of old fir forests heated by the sun,
Where drops of resin down the rough bark run,
And needle litter breathes its wonderment.
The old fir forests heated by the sun,
Their thought shall linger like the lingering scent,
Their beauty haunts us, and a wonderment
Of moss, of fern, of cones, of rills that run.
The needle litter breathes a wonderment;
The crimson crans are sparkling in the sun;
From tree to tree the scampering squirrels run;
The hum of insects blends with heat and scent.
The drops of resin down the rough bark run;
And ripe, ever riper grows the scent;
But eve has come, to end the wonderment,
And slowly up the tree trunk climbs the sun.

Eugene Lee-Hamilton

Someone's sitting in the shade today because someone planted a tree a long time ago.

Warren Buffett

Autumn
— the fulfilment

Whether you see Autumn as the 'dying' of the year or a glorious grand finale to another cycle of life in the woodland, no one can deny that it is a spectacular show – and Tollymore invariably pulls out all the stops to make it a memorable experience worth visiting year after year.

Their year's work done creating food and fuel for the tree its leaves have to be cast off as it strips down to 'hibernate' for the winter, to decay on the woodland floor and return their valuable constituents to the earth, available for re-use when needed – the ultimate lesson in recycling.

Leaves are the most amazingly complex photo-chemical factories and of the compounds involved in their work chlorophyll, which makes sugar from sunlight, is the dominant, its colour giving the leaves their varying shades of green. But as days shorten and temperatures and energy supplies fall, growth hormones stop being produced and it's time to take a break for the winter. The chlorophyll molecules break down and the colours of other chemicals (anthocyanins and carotenoids to give them names) – the yellows, reds, oranges and purples of autumn – become dominant creating the year's exuberant climax.

Summer passes into autumn in some imaginable point of time, like the turning of a leaf

Henry David Thoreau (1817-1862)

Apart from genetic differences between tree species a number of factors affect the autumn colouring of leaves – and its intensity. One of the functions of these other chemicals is to protect the delicate chlorophyll from

excessively intense sunlight, so the hotter and brighter it is during late summer and early autumn the more of them are produced and the finer the autumn display will be! The timing of the autumn colour burst is also largely determined by weather conditions – a warm wet September and October keeps things ticking over and delays the time when the trees must shut down for the winter, but one touch of frost – and it's curtain up for the big show!

First spring, now it is autumn's turn to spread a new
patchwork of colours across the parkland

Autumn – the year's last loveliest smile

William C Bryant

143

The Footstick Bridge – and shafts of low autumn sunlight shining down from the mountain tops seem to set the autumn woods on fire

October parties above the Meeting of the Waters

October's Party

October gave a party,
The leaves by hundreds cam –
The chestnuts, oak and maples
And leaves of every name.
The sunshine spread a carpet,
And everything was grand,
Miss Weather led the dancing,
Professor Wind the band.

George Cooper

145

Uneasy accord – a grey and a red squirrel side by side forage the leaf litter for their autumn feeding

A red squirrel drops in for a free lunch at one of Tollymore's feeding stations.

The battle of the bushy-tails

Everyone's favourite woodland animal, the red squirrel, which became extinct in the 1660s as a result of hunting and the removal of Ireland's once coast-to-coast woodland cover, was re-introduced in south County Down about 160 years ago and first appeared in Tollymore in 1880. It spread and flourished for just over a century before going into an almost terminal decline following the arrival of its introduced alien rival, the grey squirrel. Over recent years it has been re-introduced in Tollymore and a group of volunteers, the Tollymore Red Squirrel Group, with the support of the Forest Service, the Mourne Heritage Trust, the NI Environment Agency and others, are working to ensure its long term survival by maintaining special 'reds only' feeding stations strategically located throughout the woods. They are now numbered in the hundreds and there are high hopes of long term survival, but vigilance will always have to be maintained.

The reds and the greys have two different feeding requirements so with its diversity Tollymore should be able to accommodate both, unfortunately the grey (which can also be destructive of young trees) carries a disease, squirrel poxvirus, which has been blamed for the reduction in red populations. While a sharp eye can see shy reds travelling through the high branches (their preferred mode of travel) ones seen foraging on the ground and scampering up the tree trunks – fairly seldom now – will more likely be the grey.

Red squirrels are seed eaters favouring pine, larch and spruce cones. They also enjoy fungi, shoots and fruits of shrubs and trees (and sometimes birds' eggs). They do not hibernate and store fungi for the winter months. Greys favour bigger seeds such as acorn and beech nuts and can find richer pickings in broad-leaved woodlands, where they can survive at densities maybe eight times that of reds.

Leaves

Peace to these little broken leaves,
That strew our common ground;
That chase their tails, like silly dogs,
As they go round and round.
For though in winter boughs are bare,
Let us not once forget
Their summer glory, when these leaves
Caught the great Sun in their strong net;
And made him, in the lower air,
Tremble - no bigger than a star!

W.H. Davies

Drifting autumn leaves form patterns
across the surface of the Mill Ponds

Autumn is a second spring,
when every leaf is a flower.

Albert Camus

There is a pleasure in the pathless woods

Byron

A woodland in full colour is awesome
as a forest fire, in magnitude at least,
but a single tree is like a dancing
tongue of flame to warm the heart.

Hal Borland (1900 – 1978)

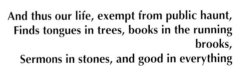

And thus our life, exempt from public haunt,
Finds tongues in trees, books in the running
brooks,
Sermons in stones, and good in everything

Shakespeare – As You Like It

We must protect the forests for our children, grandchildren and children yet to be born. We must protect the forests for those who can't speak for themselves such as the birds, animals, fish and trees.

Qwatsinas (Hereditary Chief Edward Moody), Nuxalk Nation

A fungi foray

Weird and wonderful or just strange and sometimes scary, a foray through the Tollymore undergrowth in autumn and early winter will reveal an unbelievable array of mushrooms and toadstools of all shapes, sizes and colours – the fruiting bodies of fungi. They are all you see because the business end of the organism consists of barely visible threads forming a cobweb-like net that spreads not just though the soil but through the wood of living and of course fallen trees.

There are some 6,000 species of fungi in the British Isles. Some are parasitic of living trees, most, known as saprophytes, live on dead material, all obtaining nourishment and energy by breaking down complex substances. Although they invade and can lead to the decay and eventually death of trees, the entire woodland ecosystem would collapse without them – their activities underpin everything, from the 'recycling' of dead material – they 'soften up' timber to let insects and beetles get to work – to working in symbiosis with root systems to make nutrients available to growing trees (it is reckoned that the total mass of fungi threads around the root system of a beech tree could weigh more than the tree itself).

Once a year they put their heads above the parapet so to speak with a mind-boggling variety of shapes sizes and colours of the spore-producing bodies we see as toadstools. As many are very selective in the type of woodland they like

to associate with the toadstools you can find change according to the part of the park you are in and the trees you walk among. They grow from the ground, form brackets on the trunks of trees and of course burst out in profusion from fallen branches and dead stumps. Some are elegant and shapely and colourful, some seem sinister. Only very few of the toadstools are serious poisoners, but it's best not to take chances!

The Story
of the park

The valley of the Shimna, with steep mountain slopes to the south and gently dipping fields to the north, has evolved through many changes since a bear scooped salmon from the river, a wolf lapped its water and wild boar snuffled through the woodland floor. Many hands, many generations, have played their part in creating the present landscape of managed forest and lawns that is Tollymore Forest Park.

Where the visitor now stands on the rocky edge of a deep pool, the early hunter once stood to spear, and later net, the fish to feed his family. The mixed natural woodland and scrub that clothed all the land except the mountain heights provided nuts and berries to supplement the diet. Later, when animals were herded rather than hunted and land was turned to growing crops, the ancient woodland was virtually cleared, enclosed fields and mountain heath replacing it.

Tollymore was home to extended communities in the Bronze Age. The King's Grave, as it is called, at the west side of the park, is a typical burial cairn of the times, between 1500 and 1000 BC, which were also territorial markers for tribal lands. Sadly now allowed

The Horn Bridge, with its wooden walkway astride the stream that flows through the Pleasure Gardens. It was built in 1780 and carries the driveway, from the west, that was originally the main entrance to the demesne when the family's main estate was at Dundalk

to have been almost obliterated by scrub, but once a fine example of a large Iron Age ring fort, the White Fort in the forest was a typical walled homestead enclosure probably from between 100 and 500 AD showing that the land was an important farming area probably

The Monument – a 25 feet high granite obelisk erected by the Second Earl of Roden in memory of his second son James who died in 1812 at the age of 23.

supporting a community of hundreds.

Such homesteads were often inhabited until almost the middle ages. Generation after generation made their marks on the landscape of which few traces remain, and patterns of boundaries were established defining properties and dynasties which became powerful political forces in what were turbulent times.

Tollymore makes its first appearance in the written records in 1611 when it was part of a large grant of land to Bryan Magennis, head of the powerful Irish clan that had for generations controlled most of south Down. (Granting a right to continue to occupy their own lands was a technique favoured by the Crown to ensure the local chieftains toed the English line)

At this time and for many years after the land was not improved or cultivated but left rough for grazing sheep and goats and deer hunting, being described 1674 as consisting of 500 acres of open woodland, and 300 acres each of gorse and heath and of moorland.

The estate had passed through marriage in the 1660s to the Hamilton family of Scottish descent but Tollymore was on the periphery of the family's interests, except as a 'weekend retreat' for hunting and recreation and it was two generations later in the early 18th century that the potential of its setting began to be realised and the programme of improvements that led to it becoming one of the finest demesnes in the north of Ireland got under way.

William Hamilton's grandson James (who later became Lord Limerick), began to develop the deer park around about 1710, building proper boundary walls, laying out 'ridings and vistas' and in 1726 built the first permanent stone bridge across the Shimna, the New Bridge, immediately south of what is now the car park, which opened up the land south of the river for access by carts and carriages.

He also started a major planting of trees, but probably for their amenity rather than commercial value, the first steps in the evolution of a parkland in which the landscape's natural assets would be allowed to predominate, a 'revolutionary' idea at the time and largely the result of the influence of pioneering architect Thomas

Wright, who also inspired the informal design of most of the buildings in the park.

By the middle of the 18th century the transition from deer park (the deer were still there but rather more confined) to demesne and plantation was well under way, work had started on a more substantial house and the first exotic trees and flowering shrubs were rooting in the arboretum. Much of the park south of the river and over the hills was still rough ground and pasture.

Lord Limerick (by then also Earl of Clanbrassil) died in 1758, succeeded by his son James, the Second Earl of Clanbrassil, who over the next 40 years created most of the features of the park we see today. Most of the structures, charming and quaint, familiar to Tollymore visitors were created by him – the contrasting Barbican and Bryansford gates (now the entrance and exit gates respectively), the church-like Clanbrassil Barn building with its clock tower, the Hermitage by the river, and no fewer than five new stone bridges over the Shimna, including probably one of the best-loved and charming features of the park, Foley's Bridge.

He also created a five-acre walled kitchen garden, with large glass-houses, and laid out with fruit trees and bushes and vegetable and flower beds. It is now the upper car park.

But it was the Second Earl's passion for tree planting and vision for the economic potential of commercial forestry that really changed the landscape. He contin-

The barn that looks like a church! The Clanbrassil Barn was built between about 1760 and 1785, probably in stages, originally just as a barn and later embellished with its clock tower and steeple. Until the late 1960s it the ground floor was used as stables and the upper floor as a corn store. In the nineteenth century its bell was rung at the starting and finishing time of the working day and to mark family occasions

ued his father's planting on the north side of the river but now extended his conifer plantations on the southern hill slopes, setting the pattern for the present forest. In the 12 years between 1777 and 1789 he planted almost 340,000 trees, mostly oak, spruce, silver fir and Scots pine. He also planted more than 25,000 larch which in the following century would gain Tollymore a reputation of producing the best of this timber – of major importance for boat building – in the British Isles.

He also continued to expand the seven acres of arbo-

The Ivy Bridge (also at times known as the Clanbrassil Bridge and the New Bridge) was one of the five the Second Earl constructed. A wide bridge, its parapets elegantly curve out with their ends marked by four quaint towers. Prior to the Earl's endeavours the only stone bridge, built in 1726, was the 'Old Bridge' immediately south of the car park

The Ivy Bridge clothed as befits its name

retum and pleasure gardens with new rare and exotic specimens.

Clanbrassil died in 1798, without children, and Tollymore passed via his sister to the Jocelyn family, the Earls of Roden. In 1802 the house, now a large mansion, became the family's main residence (Clanbrassil's 'seat' had been his 6,000-acre estate at Dundalk) and Robert, the Second Earl, continued a programme of improvements to the amenities of the demesne, including 26 acres of fenced deer park on either side of what is now the main drive. A number of small summer houses and iron suspension bridges across the river were constructed but have not survived.

Tree planting also continued and through the early decades of the nineteenth century the earlier plantings began progressively to reach maturity and timber production became increasingly important in what was a working estate. A saw-mill, driven by water taken from a weir across the Shimna (where the Footstick Bridge now is) was built in 1828; its foundations can still be seen by the Mill Ponds below the Lake. The Lake itself was created several decades later as a reservoir to enhance the supply. It was fed by an artificial channel, more than a mile long, dug diagonally across the hillsides to draw water from the Cascade River where it enters the park on its southern boundary. Its course can still be traced.

Miles of roads that visitors now use as they walk through Tollymore were built at this time to facilitate timber extraction.

Many of the drainage ditches running through the forest, and the southern boundary wall separating it from the open mountainside were created during the Great Famine in the 1840s as relief schemes to provide work for the destitute. The Third Earl of Roden was an exemplary landlord at this time, providing food for starving families and paid work on the estate.

He died in 1870 and over the next 45 years there was a succession of four fairly short-lived earldoms, none of whom seem to have shared the commitment of their predecessors for the continued development or enhancement of the estate. Commercial forestry operations continued; in fact with the industrial revolution, the burgeoning mining industry and the urbanisation of Britain and Northern Ireland demand for timber was insatiable. It is likely that by the end of the century more trees were being harvested than were being planted – a downward spiral.

In 1898 members of the Incorporated Gas Institute of Great Britain made a tour of Northern Ireland which included a visit to Tollymore. A note in their itinerary (written by Robert Lloyd Praeger) said:

> 'Tollymore Park is still a lovely spot, although the wholesale cutting of fine timber has greatly shorn it of the beauty which it possessed a quarter of a century ago … it awakes in those who remember it then a feeling of sadness when they consider to what extent the glory has departed.'

The demands of the First World War saw wholesale felling of much of the commercial forest and the Eighth Earl, who had inherited in 1915, had little interest in growing trees, or in much else about Tollymore, with the result that hundreds of acres were left to revert to scrubland. Fortunately the gardens and arboretum

This charming little stone rustic bridge crosses the Azalea Walk stream just before it enters the Shimna

years of experience of successful timber production and records of what grew best and where. First the south side of the Drinns and the area known as the White Plains, which had been left unplanted for grazing, were planted with larch, beech and Scots pine. Then during the 1930s the scrub areas were cleared and replanted and, with some interruptions such as the Second World War (when most of the remaining trees that were big enough were felled and driven into the sands along Dundrum Bay as coastal defences), the cycles of felling and planting as the trees reach maturity were established that are the pattern for the forest today.

Some forestry practices have changed however. The progressive thinning out of plantations as the trees grow for instance, shown in a series of catastrophic gales in the 1950s (from which Tollymore itself escaped fairly lightly) to increase the risk of them being blown down by strong winds, is no longer carried out, the law of the survival of the strongest being allowed to take its course.

fared better in that the Earl's wife was knowledgeable and enthusiastic about landscaping and invested time and resources into the planting and cultivation of trees and shrubs.

Fortunately in the late 1920s Northern Ireland's new Government came into the market for land for a planned massive expansion of state forestry operations and in 1929 it paid a relieved Earl £6 an acre for the 808 acres of Tollymore south of the river and the west end of the park.

Tollymore was a dream purchase for the foresters of the time because unlike the 'blasted heaths' that were being purchased elsewhere for tree planting the Park had 200

But the Second World War was the catalyst for the last great event in the transition of Tollymore from feudal deer park to the most popular public park in Northern Ireland. At the outbreak, in common with many other stately homes, the big house was offered to the Government as a hospital and in1940 was occupied by 250 military medical staff, the family separating off part of one of the wings for their private use. However the erection of camp kitchens on the lawns and Nissen huts below where the caravan and camping site now are proved too much for the Earl and he persuaded the

Minister of Agriculture to pay £10,000 for the house and the remaining 383 acres, re-uniting the gardens and the plantations.

After 12 years of 'No entry' status (except with written permission) as a state forest the decision was taken that Tollymore should be opened as a public forest park, the first in Northern Ireland. The derelict house was demolished to make a car park (you walk on its remains when you ramble along some of the forest roads), tarmac driveways and new riverside paths were laid down, lawns and shrubs were manicured and, on 2nd June 1955, to bands playing and flags waving, the Governor of Northern Ireland Lord Wakehurst opened Tollymore Forest Park to the people.

The wall that marks the southern boundary of the demesne with the mountain moorland was built as a relief scheme to help ease the penury of the local families during the famine of the 1840s

Find out more

A detailed and fascinating account of how a patch of mountain scrubland, first mentioned in the written records exactly 400 years ago, became Tollymore Forest Park, one of Ireland's most scenic and popular outdoor recreation areas, has been excellently told in *Tollymore – The Story of an Irish Demesne* written by the Earl of Roden and published by the Ulster Architectural Heritage Society. Set against the background of a changing and often tumultuous social and political environment it brings to life the successive generations of its stewardship, the families who managed and developed it and the heritage they created.

There are many books of course on how woodlands work and what goes on in them but a number of organisations have excellently informative web sites. Among them are:

The Royal Forestry Society (www.rfs.org.uk), the Woodland Trust (www.woodland-trust.org.uk) and Trees for Life (www.treesforlife.org.uk). Many see and seek spirituality in trees and they can find many uplifting items in www.spiritoftrees.org. The Forest Service of Northern Ireland of course has an informative website including full details of its policies, facilities and plans, and including a detailed history of the development of forestry in Northern Ireland (www.forestserviceni.gov.uk).

The building of hermitages and fanciful retreats was a popular fashion of the time and when Lord Clanbrassil's good friend the Marquis de Monthermer, (about whom nothing is known now) died in 1770 he created a memorial to him in the form of the famous Hermitage, which seems to grow out of the living rock wall of the Shimna gorge

The Hermitage steps are a good place for the autumn leaves to gather and chatter

Bridges were not only built across the big rivers; even tiny streams and drainage channels offered opportunities for whimsical and eccentric exercises of stonemason's skill. Here an enterprising tree uses the little bridge to send its roots across an old drainage channel

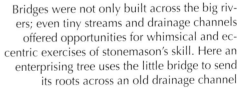

The remains of an 18th Century lime kiln, beside the stream that passes under the entrance drive, which was built to produce the mortar for the many buildings and bridges that were built during the second half of the century and probably also fertiliser for the vegetable gardens

Known as one of 'Clanbrassil's follies' this picturesque tower by the side of the road west of
Bryansford was originally a pedestrian entrance to
the Park but its doorway has long been blocked up

Latch of the gate that opened from the walled
garden (now the upper car park) to the arboretum

The Third Earl of Roden was a man of evangelical fervour and was master of Tollymore from 1820 to 1870. The flat face of this great split granite boulder, left near the river's edge by a glacier grinding down from the Mournes 20,000 years ago, offered the perfect opportunity for him to express his appreciation of the beauty he saw around him and he had it inscribed with the verse from John's Gospel – 'Stop, look around and praise the name of him who made it all'

Believer or non-believer, few are likely to quarrel with that sentiment.

Cottage

Publications

For more information and to see our other titles, please visit our website
www.cottage-publications.com
or alternatively you can contact us as follows:–

Telephone: +44 (0)28 9188 8033
Fax: +44 (0)28 9188 8063

Cottage Publications
is an imprint of
Laurel Cottage Ltd.,
15 Ballyhay Road,
Donaghadee, Co. Down,
N. Ireland, BT21 0NG